Watch it Grow

Mouse

Barrie Watts

W

FRANKLIN WATTS
LONDON•SYDNEY

This edition 2007
First published in 2003 by Franklin Watts
338 Euston Road, London NW1 3BH

Franklin Watts Australia
Level 17/207 Kent Street, Sydney, NSW 2000

© Barrie Watts 2003

Editor: Jackie Hamley
Art director: Jonathan Hair
Photographer: Barrie Watts
Reading consultant: Beverley Mathias

A CIP catalogue record for this book
is available from the British Library

ISBN 978 0 7496 7359 8

Dewey classification: 599.35'3

Printed in China

Franklin Watts is a divison of Hachette Children's Books.

How to use this book

Watch It Grow has been specially designed to cater for a
range of reading and learning abilities. Initially children may
just follow the pictures. Ask them to describe in their own
words what they see. Other children will enjoy reading the
single sentence in large type, in conjunction with the pictures.
This single sentence is then expanded in the main text. More
adept readers will be able to follow the text and pictures by
themselves through to the conclusion of the life cycle.

Contents

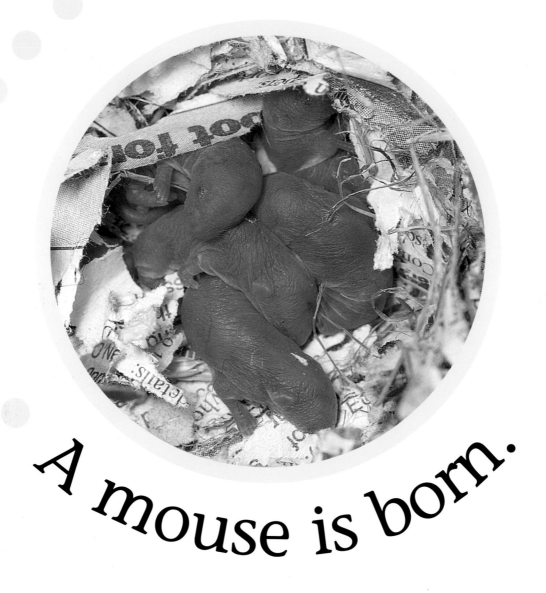

A mouse is born.

These baby mice have just been born. Each one is about the size of a grape. They cannot hear or see. They have no fur, so their mother keeps them warm in a nest.

The mice are too small to eat solid food. Their mother feeds them on rich milk from **teats** on her stomach. This is called **suckling**. Animals that **suckle** their young are called **mammals**.

The fur starts to grow.

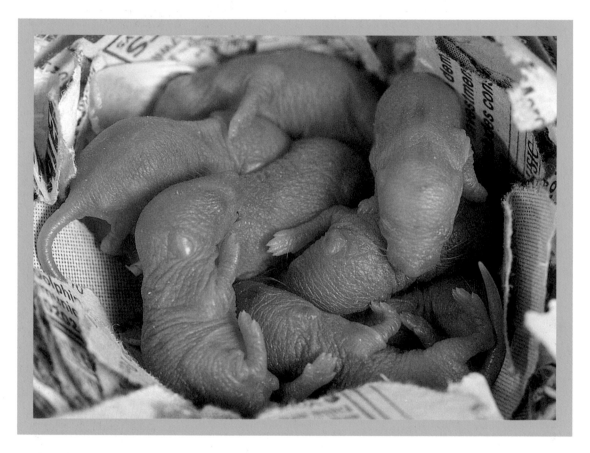

After four days, the pink skin of the baby mice starts to turn grey. Their fur is beginning to grow beneath their skin. It takes about 10 days to come through.

By the time the baby mice are 14 days old, they have a thick coat of fur. It keeps them warm when their mother leaves the nest to look for food.

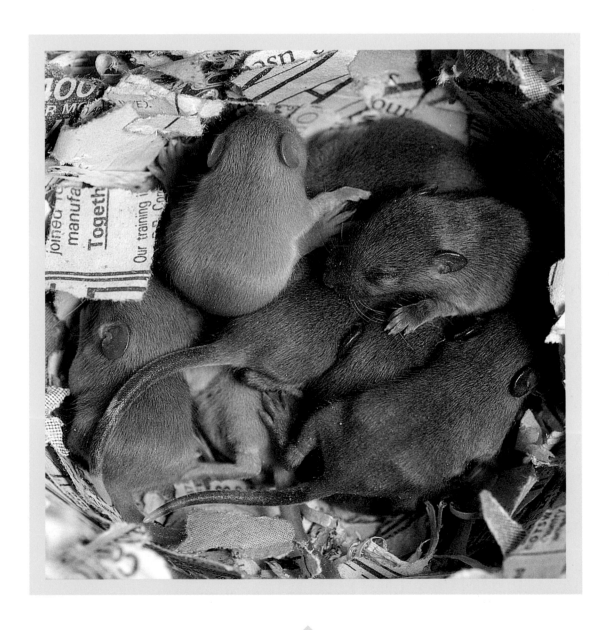

The eyes begin to open.

When the baby mice are born, their eyes are covered in a thin layer of skin. After about two weeks, their eyes begin to open. They do not open their eyes fully straight away because the bright light hurts them.

Gradually, the baby mice open their eyes until they can see properly. At first their eyes look like small slits, but after a week they can open them wide.

The mouse eats solid food.

As the young mouse grows, it needs more food. Its teeth have got harder and it begins to eat solid food, such as nuts and seeds. Its mother feeds it less milk and she starts to bring food to the nest. This is called **weaning**.

As soon as the young mouse eats solid food, it begins to look outside the nest for its own food.

The mouse comes out of the nest.

About five weeks after being born, the young mouse comes out of the nest. At first, the mouse is weak. It crawls about slowly and stays close to the nest.

As it gets more exercise, the mouse becomes stronger. Gradually, it moves further away to look for its own food, but it still comes back to the nest often.

The mouse cleans itself.

The mouse's fur keeps it warm in cold weather. Dirt and tiny creatures such as **fleas** harm the fur, so the mouse makes sure it is clean and tidy.

The mouse uses its front paws
to clean its fur. It licks them and
then rubs them all over its body,
from the tip of its nose to the
end of its tail.

The mouse can climb well.

In its search for food, the mouse
will climb, jump or even swim.
If it lives indoors, it climbs up
curtains or into cupboards to
look for food.

The mouse uses its long tail to balance itself. When it is cold, the mouse can climb up the outside wall of a house to reach the warm **loft** where it will spend the winter.

The mouse uses its ears and nose.

The mouse is mostly active during the night when many people are asleep. Young mice cannot see very well, but they have excellent hearing. Their large ears can easily pick up small noises.

Mice have a good sense of smell, too. They are always sniffing the air in case **predators** are nearby. Even so, mice are often eaten by **nocturnal** creatures such as cats.

The mouse is fully grown.

After three months the mouse is almost as big as its mother and ready to **mate**. The nest is too small for all the brothers and sisters, so the mouse leaves to look for a home of its own.

Male mice often travel far from
the nest where they grew up.
If they stayed too near the nest,
they would fight with other
males in the area.

The male and female mate.

When the mouse has found a new home, it prepares to **mate**. The female will only **mate** with the male when she is ready to have babies. If he tries before she is ready, she chases him away.

When the mice **mate**, they are only together for one day. The male leaves the female and she will care for the babies.

The female gets fatter.

A week after **mating**, the female's stomach starts to swell. She is **pregnant** and her babies are growing inside her.

When the female is **pregnant** she needs lots of food and water. Her weight more than doubles and she becomes very fat. She is unable to run and gets tired easily.

The female makes a nest.

About 18 days after **mating**, the female makes a nest where she will have her babies. She chooses a warm, safe place.

She lines the nest with things she finds close to her home, such as newspaper, dried grass and chewed fabric. As the babies grow bigger inside her, she makes the rich milk that she will use to **suckle** them.

The young are born.

The female gives birth 20 days after **mating**. As each baby is born, she cleans it by licking it all over. She can give birth to as many as 10 young, which are born one after the other.

The female stays with them in the nest and rests. She keeps the babies warm and takes care of them until they are old enough to start looking after themselves.

Word bank

Fleas - small insects that feed on the blood of another animal. Fleas can jump from one animal to another.

Loft - the area at the top of a house, beneath the roof. Lofts are often very warm.

Mammals - animals that are warm-blooded and feed their babies with milk from their own bodies. Humans, cats, dogs, horses, cows and mice are all mammals.

Mate, Mating - when the female mouse and the male mouse come together to make babies.

Nocturnal - animals that are nocturnal are mostly active during the night.

Predators - animals that hunt and eat other animals. Cats and birds are a mouse's main predators.

Pregnant - when a female has babies growing inside her.

Suckle, Suckling - when a mother feeds her babies with milk from her body.

Teats - nipples on a female animal from which milk comes out.

Weaning - when babies stop feeding on milk from their mother and start eating solid food.

Life cycle

When they are born, baby mice have no fur and cannot hear, see or eat solid food.

Two days later, the mouse gives birth.

After four days, the fur starts to grow beneath the skin.

Eighteen days after mating, the pregnant female makes a nest.

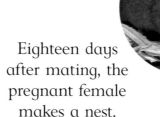

Ten days later, the fur has grown and the mouse starts to open its eyes.

Twelve weeks after being born, the mouse is fully grown and looks for a new home.

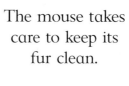

The young mouse eats solid food and looks for food outside the nest.

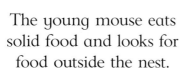

The mouse takes care to keep its fur clean.

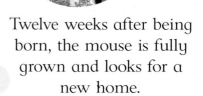

Index